What Was
Stonewall?

by Nico Medina

illustrated by Jake Murray

Penguin Workshop

For Billy—and for the tribe—with gratitude to
those who paved the way—NM

For Andrew, John, and Dani—JM

PENGUIN WORKSHOP
An Imprint of Penguin Random House LLC, New York

Library of Congress Cataloging-in-Publication Data is available upon request.

ISBN 9781524786007 (paperback)   10 9 8 7 6 5 4 3 2 1
ISBN 9781524786021 (library binding)   10 9 8 7 6 5 4 3 2 1

Contents

What Was Stonewall? 1

The Village 7

Before 16

Welcome to the Stonewall Inn 34

"Police! We're Taking the Place!" 40

Uprising 50

Organizing 61

Crisis 78

Out and Proud 88

The Struggle Continues 96

Timelines 104

Bibliography 106

Resources 107

What Was Stonewall?

June 26, 2015—Greenwich Village, New York City

It was a Friday, and folks at the Stonewall Inn were celebrating. The world-famous gay bar was packed. People hugged and cheered inside the bar and outside on Christopher Street.

Everyone had come to celebrate a ruling from the Supreme Court, the highest court in the United States. Now it was legal, in all fifty states, for same-sex couples to marry. "They ask for equal dignity in the eyes of the law," wrote Justice Anthony Kennedy. "The Constitution grants them that right."

Marriage is important not only for emotional reasons but for practical reasons as well. Married people can own property together, and they pay lower taxes. They can also be covered under the same health insurance plan and can visit each other in the hospital. These are just some of the many legal benefits of being married.

Up until 2004, men could only marry women in the United States, and vice versa. But beginning that year, states started to recognize every American's right to marry whomever they chose.

By June 2015, same-sex marriage was legal in thirty-seven states, plus the District of Columbia.

The Supreme Court's decision now gave the right to marry to all Americans.

Many LGBTQ+ people had been waiting for this moment for a long time.

To see the Stonewall Inn, one might wonder what makes it so special. From the outside, it is not a particularly pretty establishment. Inside, the ceilings are low and the bar is dark. Why did so many New Yorkers celebrate there?

Because almost fifty years earlier, something happened at Stonewall. Something that would change the course of history for LGBTQ+ Americans.

On June 28, 1969, police raided the Stonewall Inn and began arresting people. This had happened many times before, at Stonewall and at other gay-friendly bars in the city. But on that hot summer night, to the cops' surprise, the people at Stonewall fought back.

And they fought back hard.

What Does It Mean to Be LGBTQ+ (Lesbian, Gay, Bisexual, Transgender, Queer, Plus)?

Love and *identity*—what makes someone who they are—take many forms:

Lesbian: a woman whose physical, romantic, emotional attraction is to other women. The word *lesbian* comes from the Greek island of Lesbos, where the poet Sappho lived and wrote about the beauty of women.

Gay: people whose physical, romantic, emotional attractions are to people of the same sex. Gay people (both gay men and lesbians) have also been referred to as *homosexual*, but that term is considered aggressive and offensive today. ("Straight" people, who are attracted to the opposite sex, are also known as *heterosexual*.)

Bisexual: someone who forms physical, romantic, emotional attractions to more than one gender.

Transgender: people whose *gender* (how they feel on the inside, and how they express themselves) is different from the *sex* (male or female) they had or were assigned when they were born. Some trans people decide to undergo surgery or other medical treatment so their outward appearance matches their true self.

Queer: once considered an offensive term, some people have reclaimed it to refer to any identity that is not strictly heterosexual. Some queer people prefer to be called "they" instead of "he" or "she."

Then there are some people (*+/Plus*) who don't feel that any of these categories fully describe them.

In 2016, an estimated ten million Americans—about 4 percent of the population—identified as LGBTQ+.

The struggle for equal rights for LGBTQ+ people did not begin at Stonewall. But the events there pushed the movement forward. Half a century later, Stonewall continues to inspire people to demand equality.

Stonewall Inn, present day

CHAPTER 1
The Village

Stonewall is located in New York City's Greenwich Village neighborhood (say: GREN-itch). Commonly called "the Village," its winding streets and small parks set it apart from the rectangular street grid in the rest of the city.

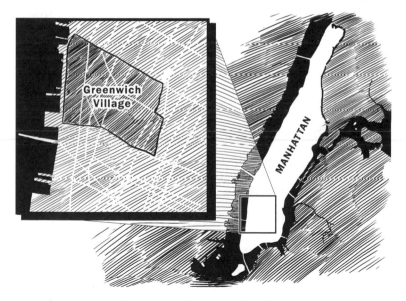

Manhattan and Greenwich Village

Walt Whitman

The Village has been a popular place for gay people to gather since the 1800s. Pfaff's was an underground saloon where gay men met, including the famous poet Walt Whitman.

In the early 1900s, the Village was the center of New York's bohemian culture. (To be *bohemian* means to be unusual and accepting of those who are different.) Poets, musicians, and other artistic types from around the city—and the country—flocked to the area.

Some of these newcomers were queer. These people found more acceptance here than they did elsewhere. Still, many couldn't live an open life. Outside the Village—and even within it—they faced disapproval and discrimination.

But queer culture blossomed nonetheless. Dazzling costume balls featuring drag queens were held across the Village and other downtown neighborhoods. (A *drag queen* is a man who dresses and performs as a woman.) From 1869 through the 1920s, drag balls were also held in the uptown African American neighborhood of Harlem.

Drag ball at Webster Hall

Strike a Pose

The 1980s saw the rise of a new kind of ball in Harlem: the vogue ball. Voguers part-walked, part-danced down a runway. They moved their hands and arms in dramatic and expressive ways. They also dropped into beautiful or difficult poses to show how athletic they were. In some ways, it is similar to break dancing. Sometimes voguers competed in downtown New York clubs. It was there that pop icon Madonna was inspired to write her best-selling song "Vogue."

When the United States entered World War I in 1917, American soldiers sailed to Europe from New York City. Many visited Greenwich Village before shipping off. Perhaps for the first time ever, they saw openly queer people.

Many American women moved to cities like New York to fill the jobs left open by the soldiers. In these lively places, away from home and the pressure to marry and raise children, some women realized that they were gay.

Meanwhile, queer American soldiers stationed overseas might have visited cities like Paris and Berlin, where queer culture was even more open than it was in New York. When they returned to the United States, some men began a new life— and many settled in the Village.

A lesbian culture developed in cities like New York. *Drag kings*—women who dressed and performed as men—appeared in nightclubs. Private apartment parties featuring dancing and jazz music became popular. A'Lelia Walker, a wealthy black heiress in Harlem, became famous for her legendary parties. Some were attended by European and African royalty!

A'Lelia Walker

During Prohibition (1920–1933), the manufacture and sale of alcohol was illegal in the United States. Secret bars serving alcohol, called *speakeasies*, began to open.

Some speakeasies catered to queer people. Eve's Hangout was popular with lesbians. A sign on its door read: "Men are admitted but not welcome."

The original Stonewall Inn opened in 1930 on Seventh Avenue South. (It moved to Christopher Street in 1934.) It called itself a tearoom but was actually a speakeasy.

Prohibition may have made queer life easier. Because bars had to operate in secret, queer people had relatively safe and private places to get together. But by the end of the 1920s, queer

Mae West

life in New York was becoming less free and accepted. *The Drag* was a play written by a famous actress named Mae West. The play featured a drag ball and other queer themes. It was banned before it opened on Broadway. New York State passed a law forbidding such subjects onstage.

The drag balls were shut down, too. Cross-dressing—dressing in the traditional clothing of the opposite sex—was outlawed.

After Prohibition ended in 1933, bars were required to have a liquor license from the state government. But the government wouldn't give licenses to bars that served queer people.

After the good times of the Roaring Twenties came the Great Depression. Times were tough, and with nowhere left to go, queer people went back to living in the shadows.

CHAPTER 2
Before

In 1950s America, gay people could be arrested for kissing or for holding hands in public. This behavior was against the law in all fifty states. Most Americans supported these laws. Sometimes police officers pretended to be gay in order to arrest gay people who asked them on dates.

Newspapers published the names and addresses of people arrested for being queer. This was called being *outed*. As a result, a person might get fired, kicked out of their home, or worse. Outed people were forced to leave the armed forces. Gay people could not work for the US government.

It's not surprising that most queer people lived their lives in secret—"in the closet."

Being "Out" in the Workplace Today

In many places today, it is still legal to fire people—or refuse to hire them—because they are LGBTQ+. The Employee Non-Discrimination Act (ENDA) is a bill that has come before Congress many times. ENDA would make it illegal nationwide for employers to discriminate against anyone beca of their gender or identity. It has never become law.

As for the military, a 1993 law called Don't Ask, Don't Tell (DADT) finally allowed gay people to serve in the armed forces—as long as they kept their sexuality a secret. In 2010, the US Congress and President Barack Obama decided to end DADT.

In 2017, President Donald J. Trump announced the military would no longer allow transgender people to serve. This policy is being challenged in the courts.

For a very long time, doctors claimed that homosexuality was a mental illness. They also believed that this "disorder" could be "cured" through psychotherapy. Some queer people were forced by their families into mental hospitals for "treatment."

Some doctors used horrible methods to try to make gay people straight. Male patients had their private parts removed in surgery. Others were given electric shocks and lobotomies, a kind of brain surgery. Lobotomies often resulted in severe brain damage, and even death.

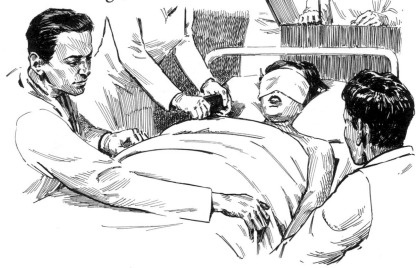

Conversion Therapy

Also known as "reparative therapy," gay conversion therapy claims to "cure" a person of their same-sex attraction through prayer, talk therapy, and other methods. American psychological and medical associations say the practice does not work. They say it harms rather than helps patients, and many ex-patients agree. As of November 2018, there were laws against conversion therapy in fourteen states, plus the District of Columbia. (Religious and spiritual leaders, however, can continue to perform this kind of therapy.)

Today, procedures such as lobotomies are, for the most part, no longer accepted by the medical community.

Some young LGBTQ+ people chose to run away from home rather than face such "medical" practices. Others were thrown out by their families. They flocked to queer-friendly neighborhoods in cities across the country: San Francisco. Los Angeles. Chicago. Washington, DC. And, of course, New York City.

Many gay and transgender kids in the Village ended up on the streets. Some strutted around the neighborhood dressed in drag, carrying switchblades for protection. These newcomers met other people who understood their struggles. They made friends and created new families where everyone belonged.

As LGBTQ+ youth moved to big cities, adult gay *activists* (people who work for causes they believe in) were raising awareness for gay rights.

Harry Hay was a thirty-eight-year-old gay man in Los Angeles. He founded the Mattachine Society in 1950. The name came from a group of masked performers in medieval France who never revealed their identities.

Mattachine was a kind of "secret society" for gay men. Members met in private homes. They closed the windows and drew the curtains. Only first names were used.

They met to discuss the questions on many gay men's minds: Did something cause people to be gay? Why was it viewed so negatively? Could gay people ever lead happy lives?

A few years later, the Daughters of Bilitis was founded by Del Martin and Phyllis Lyon, a lesbian couple. It began as a social club for San Francisco lesbians. But the group soon became involved in education and politics. They published a monthly magazine called *The Ladder*.

Phyllis Lyon and Del Martin

Local chapters of the Mattachine Society and Daughters of Bilitis began to open in cities across the country. They focused less on achieving equal rights and more on winning acceptance from general society. Sometimes the two groups worked together.

Dr. Franklin Kameny, an astronomer for the US Army, did not think their tactics went far enough. After Kameny was fired for being gay, he opened a chapter of the Mattachine Society in Washington, DC, in 1961. A man of science, Dr. Kameny rejected the so-called "evidence" that

Dr. Franklin Kameny

homosexuality was an illness. Queer people were *not* sick, he said. He encouraged others to stand up and say the same.

By this time, gay-rights groups had begun to come out of the shadows. Inspired by the peaceful protests of the civil rights movement, they picketed the White House and the Pentagon to protest the government's antigay policies.

Civil Rights Movement

Beginning in the 1950s, activists began to use nonviolent protest to push for equality for African Americans. Black people in Montgomery, Alabama, refused to ride city buses for more than a year. This began after Rosa Parks was arrested for not giving her seat to a white man. In 1960, black students in North Carolina sat at "whites only" lunch counters until they were served (or dragged out). This led to more sit-ins and marches across the South. Protesters sometimes faced violence, but their actions led to important changes: the Civil Rights Act of 1964 and the Voting Rights Act of 1965.

New York Mattachine member Craig Rodwell wanted to do more than join picket lines. So beginning in 1965, every July Fourth, he organized an "Annual Reminder" march. It went past Independence Hall in Philadelphia. The Declaration of Independence had been written and signed there in 1776. It states that "all men are created equal." Rodwell and his fellow activists wanted to tell the country: Gay people were equal to straight people.

Independence Hall in Philadelphia

The gatherings were small—at most, around forty people. Men wore suits and ties; women wore skirts or dresses. The idea was to show that gay people were just like everyone else. They marched in circles, single file; they did not kiss, hold hands, or talk.

This was probably not how Craig Rodwell preferred to dress or behave. As a young man in the Village years earlier, he and his friends wore super-tight blue jeans—and sometimes eyeliner. They loved shocking straight people. But to make changes in "polite" American society, Rodwell thought that it was smart to dress and act "respectably."

Craig Rodwell's Historic Bookstore

Born in Chicago, Craig Rodwell (1940–1993) was sent off to boarding school at age six. He earned a reputation as a troublemaker. Rodwell moved to New York City in the late 1950s. There he became involved in the Mattachine Society. Ever the rebel, Rodwell refused to use a fake name.

Craig Rodwell at the Oscar Wilde Memorial Bookshop

Rodwell wanted the Mattachine Society to open a bookstore as its headquarters. The answer was no, so he did it himself. The Oscar Wilde Memorial Bookshop opened in 1967. (Oscar Wilde, a famous Irish writer living in England, was imprisoned for being gay in 1895.) It was the first bookstore in the country dedicated to LGBTQ+ literature.

Oscar Wilde

Unlike the local gay bars, where windows were often boarded up or painted over, the bookstore was an openly queer landmark. It was often trashed. There were even death threats against Rodwell and his staff. But the bookstore remained open long after Rodwell had died.

The Mattachine Society in New York protested other injustices, too.

In New York—like many other states—bars that served "disorderly" customers could lose their liquor licenses. (To be *disorderly* means to cause trouble.) This law unfairly denied gay people the right to gather at bars.

How?

Gay people—by simply being gay—were considered "disorderly." Some bars displayed signs that read: "If you're gay, go away." But for many, bars were the only places queer people could meet other queer people.

On April 21, 1966, Craig Rodwell and two other Mattachine members decided to protest the law. They held a "Sip-In." They visited a number of New York bars with some reporters. Before asking for drinks, they declared themselves to be gay, and said they would remain "orderly."

A fourth Mattachine member joined them at

Julius'—a gay-friendly bar in the Village. Here, the bartender told the men, "You're gay. I can't serve you." The Mattachine Society filed a complaint. Their case went to court, and the next year, the law was overturned.

This was progress. But police harassment of gay bars and LGBTQ+ people continued.

Members of the New York Mattachine Society at Julius' Bar

CHAPTER 3
Welcome to the Stonewall Inn

The Stonewall Inn on Christopher Street opened as a gay bar on March 18, 1967. It was not a very nice place.

There was no sink with running water to wash the glassware. Toilets often broke. The walls were painted black. A sheet of plywood blocked the windows.

"The bar itself was a toilet," said one Stonewall regular, "but it was a refuge . . . from the street."

To get inside, patrons had to get past the bouncer. He had a view onto the sidewalk through a slit in the front door. Customers entered the bar's front room through a second set of doors. This room featured a black-plywood bar, tables, and chairs. An older crowd gathered here.

Younger patrons preferred the back room, where the jukebox played the latest hits. A racially mixed crowd of gay men, lesbians, drag queens, and trans people packed the dance floor.

Same-sex dancing in public remained illegal in New York City until 1968. But at the Stonewall, that didn't stop people from cutting loose and having fun with friends.

For all the sense of togetherness at Stonewall, the owners' interest in the bar was about one thing: money. Like most Village gay bars at the time, it was run by the Mafia—mobsters who operated in several big US cities.

Rather than get a liquor license, the Stonewall operated as a private bottle club. The liquor bottles behind the bar supposedly belonged to club members. The police knew this was only for show. Stonewall wasn't really a bottle club. But the owners bribed local cops to leave their place alone.

Graffiti outside Stonewall Inn, 1969

The Mafia also made money by blackmailing some of the Stonewall's wealthier patrons. *We know where you work*, they'd say. *Pay up, or we'll tell everyone that you're gay.*

Desperate to keep their identity a secret, a group of important bankers paid the bribes. They got the money by making illegal business deals in foreign countries. This caught the attention of the police.

Deputy Inspector Seymour Pine and Detective Charles Smythe were ordered to shut down the Stonewall. Proving blackmail charges would be difficult. But proving Stonewall was not a real bottle club would be easy.

Seymour Pine

On Tuesday, June 24, 1969, the police raided the bar and arrested some of the staff. The illegal alcohol was taken as evidence. This would help the cops build their case.

Patrons were very angry. Why were the cops raiding their special hangout? Still, the Stonewall reopened on Wednesday as if nothing had happened.

Inspector Pine knew it would take more than one raid to shut down the bar for good. He planned a second one for Friday night.

Nothing went according to plan.

CHAPTER 4
"Police! We're Taking the Place!"

Seymour Pine wanted his operation to go as smoothly as possible. He thought crooked local cops might warn the bar owners about the raid. So Pine enlisted the help of police officers from a different part of the city.

Four undercover officers—two men and two women—would go inside to observe the scene. They'd identify employees and cross-dressers for arrest, and gather evidence to help prove their case—that the bar didn't have a proper liquor license.

Pine, Smythe, and a couple of other officers—in plainclothes—would wait across the street in Christopher Park. Once the undercover officers reported back, everyone would go to the bar, flash their badges, and demand entry. Pine would call for backup, then begin to line people up to be arrested.

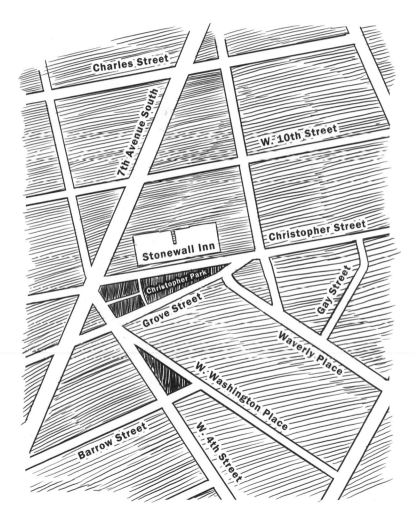

There was a full moon the night of Friday, June 27, 1969. And it was sweltering hot. The Tuesday-night raid was fresh on patrons' minds. But as Friday night turned into Saturday morning, two hundred young people were packed inside the sweaty, smoky Stonewall Inn, dancing the night away.

At 1:20 a.m., Pine pounded on the bar's front
door. "Police!" he called. "We're taking the place!"
The bouncer flashed the inside lights—the signal
for "Raid!"—before letting the cops in.

Three patrol cars arrived. Bar employees and cross-dressers were taken to the back room to be arrested. Everyone else was lined up to have their ID's checked before being released.

On their way out, hot, angry, and (in some cases) drunk bar patrons traded insults with the cops. Usually, when the cops busted a gay bar, everyone just went home. But tonight was different.

After exiting the bar, patrons waited for their friends still inside. The sidewalk became like a stage. People struck poses as they strutted out of the bar. They blew kisses and took bows. This drew cheers from the crowd, which had quickly grown to more than a hundred people.

Inside the bar, Seymour Pine and his officers were having trouble with the drag queens. Many of them were angrily resisting arrest.

A number of lesbians were fighting back, too. Cross-dressing was against the law, so women wearing men's clothing were subject to arrest. But these women would *not* go quietly.

Back outside on Christopher Street, the crowd swelled. Passersby—many of whom were queer—knew people inside. They stopped to see what was going on. Craig Rodwell was one of them.

Rumors swirled that people inside the bar were being hurt by the police. When the police

paddy wagon arrived to cart off those who'd been arrested, the crowd grew angry.

The first to be loaded into the paddy wagon were the bar owners. Some people cheered that the mobsters were under arrest. Then out came the drag queens, kicking and screaming. But there wasn't enough room inside the paddy wagon for everyone. When it filled up, the cops began loading people into patrol cars.

Eyewitness accounts vary on what happened next. But as the lesbians were removed from the bar, some officers struck the women and touched their private parts. One officer hit a lesbian in the head with a billy club.

One woman was dragged out of the bar in handcuffs. She violently resisted the cops and refused to stay in the police car. For several minutes, she fought back. Finally, she was lifted off the ground and thrown into the car!

The brutality shocked the crowd.

Bruised and bloodied, the woman screamed at the assembled crowd: "Why don't you *do* something?!"

And then they did.

CHAPTER 5
Uprising

For many in the crowd, their anger had been building for years. It was time to fight back.

"Dirty coppers!" people screamed as they pelted the police with copper pennies. Then came nickels and quarters. Then glass bottles. Cobblestones from the street. Bricks from a nearby construction site.

People ran through the streets, telling others to join the fight. They called friends on pay phones and said to get down to the Village, *pronto*!

"Pigs!" the crowd roared at the cops. They rocked the police cars and paddy wagon back and forth. They slashed tires. Craig Rodwell led a chant of "Gay power!"

Seymour Pine ordered the police cars to flee

the scene. That left him and seven others to face off against the violent mob. It was "as bad as any situation that I had met in during the army," the World War II veteran later said.

Pine's only choice was to retreat . . . back into the Stonewall. Then lock the doors and wait for backup.

This further angered the crowd. Stonewall was *theirs*—how dare the cops occupy it! The hail of bricks and bottles continued, shattering the bar's glass windows.

A team of drag queens and other men ripped a parking meter out of the sidewalk. They used it as a battering ram and busted the front door open. The crowd rained bottles and cans into the entryway.

The cops managed to shut the front door and barricade it with furniture.

Next, the protesters turned to fire. They poured cigarette-lighter fluid into glass bottles. Then they lit the bottles and hurled them into the bar's windows. A trash can full of garbage was shoved in the bar's busted windows and set aflame.

Veterans of Stonewall

Marsha P. Johnson (1945–1992) was born in New Jersey and moved to the Village in 1966. Marsha said the *P* stood for "Pay it no mind." A transgender black woman, Marsha dressed in both men's and women's clothing and modeled for the gay pop-artist Andy Warhol. The so-called "Queen of Christopher Street," Johnson was among the first to resist arrest at Stonewall.

Marsha P. Johnson and Sylvia Rivera

Sylvia Rivera (1951–2002) was a transgender Latina drag queen from New York City. She was reportedly among the first to throw a bottle at the cops. "It's the revolution!" she screamed. In 1970, along with Marsha P. Johnson, she founded STAR House to provide shelter for gay and trans kids living on the streets.

Stormé DeLarverie (1920–2014) (say: stormy de-LAR-veree) was born in New Orleans, Louisiana, to an African American mother and a white father. Stormé was a lesbian who sang and performed as a drag king. Some say Stormé threw the first punch at Stonewall. "The cop hit me, and I hit him back," she recalled. Stormé considered herself a protector of the Village lesbians. She patrolled the neighborhood into her eighties.

Stormé DeLarverie

By now, the crowd numbered more than two thousand. The officers used a fire hose to put out the flames and disperse the mob. Outside, people laughed. The water probably felt good on such a hot night!

Inside, Inspector Pine was having trouble with his radio. He couldn't call for help. Pine knew that bullets would only make things worse. So he ordered his officers not to fire their guns.

Finally, one of the female officers with Pine was able to squeeze through a ceiling vent, escape the bar, and call for backup. After forty-five minutes, thirty more officers and another paddy wagon arrived. Pine exited the bar and began arresting more people. Rioters and police clashed.

Next to arrive was the Tactical Patrol Force, or TPF—riot police. They stood shoulder to shoulder, shields in one hand, nightsticks in the other. They filled the street.

The TPF's tactics worked on the straight and uniform street grid in the rest of the city. But the Village's web of short and winding roads was confusing to them. This worked to the protesters' advantage. The Village was their home turf.

As the riot police advanced, the crowd ran around a couple of short blocks, then came on them from behind. With so many targets moving in all directions, the TPF's attention was hopelessly divided.

A few protesters—mainly drag queens—formed a chorus line and began to taunt the officers. They high-kicked and sang: "We are the Village girls / We wear our hair in curls / We wear our dungarees / Above our nelly knees." (*Nelly* is a slang term for girly or effeminate.) This was

certainly not in the TPF's training manual! The riot police began to chase down protesters. Heads were busted. There were beatings.

By 4:00 a.m., the scene had finally calmed down. Incredibly, no one had died, and just thirteen people were arrested. (Seven of them were Stonewall employees.)

The exhausted protesters were amazed and overjoyed. They had fought back against the cops. Sure, their bar was badly damaged—but the cops had retreated!

More importantly, everyone had come together—black, white, brown; gay, lesbian, trans. "We became a people," said one activist. "All of a sudden, I had brothers and sisters."

Doughnut Wars

Stonewall was not the first time LGBTQ+ people fought back. Cooper Do-nuts in Los Angeles was a popular twenty-four-hour hangout for gay men, drag queens, and trans people. In 1959, police raided the diner and arrested five people. Everyone poured into the street. They hurled doughnuts, coffee mugs, and trash at the police. The cops fled but returned with backup to beat and arrest a number of rioters.

CHAPTER 6
Organizing

Eager to keep the protest going, Craig Rodwell and his partner, Fred Sargeant, got to work. By Saturday afternoon, they had printed five thousand copies of a pamphlet. Its title was "Get the Mafia and the Cops out of Gay Bars." The pamphlet encouraged queer people to stop going to mob-owned bars, and to open their own instead.

Not everyone was happy about the run-ins with police the night before. Some older gay people preferred not to rock the boat. The Mattachine Society wrote a message on the Stonewall's boarded-up windows, pleading for peace and order.

But as far as most people were concerned, there was no going back.

The Stonewall had been destroyed. The cops had smashed all the liquor bottles, the jukebox, and the cigarette machine with baseball bats. Still, the bar reopened on Saturday.

It was another scorcher—ninety-five degrees. People gathered outside to discuss the events of the night before. Coming together. Out in the open. Organizing.

The cops returned, too, telling folks to *break it up* and *keep it moving*. Instead, the Stonewall patrons held hands and kissed. More chants rose up: "Liberate the street!" They blocked traffic, rocking cars back and forth. "Christopher Street belongs to the queens!" The demonstrations lasted until about 2:00 or 3:00 a.m.

Over the following nights, an uneasy peace settled over the Village. What would happen next?

The Fourth of July was just days away. Time for the Annual Reminder march in Philadelphia. Craig Rodwell chartered a bus, and several dozen New Yorkers joined him. In all, nearly 150 people attended, the largest such gathering yet. Major newspapers had largely ignored the Stonewall events. So Rodwell spread the word to reporters that LGBTQ+ people had declared their independence.

Some protesters broke the long-standing rules and held hands as they picketed. But Rodwell didn't care. He now hoped for a new annual march, one that would take place on the anniversary of the uprising.

Groups advocating for LGBTQ+ rights sprang up left and right. Frank Kameny, founder of the Washington, DC, Mattachine chapter, said: "By the time of Stonewall, we had fifty to sixty gay groups in the country. A year later there was at least fifteen hundred."

One month after Stonewall, more than five hundred people gathered at Washington Square Park, in the heart of the Village. They heard speeches and celebrated the progress already made. Then they marched to the Stonewall. Up till that time, it was the largest public gathering of LGBTQ+ people in American history.

The Christopher Street Gay Liberation Day march was scheduled for June 28, 1970, one year after Stonewall. Similar marches were planned in Boston, Chicago, San Francisco, and Los Angeles. Craig Rodwell's vision for a new "Annual Reminder" was coming into focus.

The New York march would start in the Village and go all the way to Central Park, about three miles away. Organizers printed maps showing where public pay phones and restrooms were located. They provided tips for safety and for keeping the peace.

The mood was tense as the march began. "Please let there be more than ten of us," one marcher remembered thinking.

How many people would be brave enough to proclaim their identity in such a public way? And it was anyone's guess what would happen once they left the safety of the Village.

As the marchers made their way uptown,

people along the sidewalks joined them. They chanted: "Two, four, six, eight—gay is just as good as straight!" And: "Three, five, seven, nine—lesbians are mighty fine!" People were not only demanding equal rights. They were saying they were proud of being gay. Soon, there were thousands of marchers. The crowd stretched for fifteen blocks. That's three-quarters of a mile!

This was truly a turning point.

The march has been held every year since. By 1979, it had doubled in size. Today, it is known as the New York City Pride March. In 2016, more than two million people lined the streets to watch and celebrate. And since 2000, the United States has recognized June as LGBTQ+ Pride Month.

Worldwide Pride

Today, LGBTQ+ pride marches are held across the globe. Cities in Germany celebrate "Christopher Street Day," named in honor of Stonewall. The city of São Paulo, Brazil, set a world record in 2009, when four million people attended its pride parade.

Pride event in Istanbul, 2015

But not all events ended happily. Pride marches in Moscow were met with anger and violence. In 2012, a Russian court banned gay celebrations for *one hundred years*. Pride events in Istanbul, Turkey, attracted one hundred thousand people in 2014. By the next year, the event had been outlawed. When people still gathered, police fired rubber bullets and water cannons at them.

Then there are some places in the world where you won't see a pride parade anytime soon. Homosexual behavior is still outlawed in many countries across Africa, the Middle East, and South Asia. In some of these places, being LGBTQ+ is punishable by death.

WorldPride is a global event that has been held in different cities around the world since 2000. In 2019, New York City will host WorldPride to commemorate the fiftieth anniversary of the Stonewall Uprising.

Stonewall and the Liberation Day marches helped usher in a new era in the fight for LGBTQ+ rights. Activists publicly pressured politicians to act on gay rights. By the end of the 1970s, cities from Seattle to Miami had passed laws protecting gay people in the workplace.

In 1975, the federal government stopped firing employees who were openly gay. Frank Kameny, the army scientist who had been fired from his job, said that the US government had finally "surrendered."

Activists worked with straight politicians to help their causes. Soon, openly gay politicians were winning elections from Michigan to Massachusetts. Frank Kameny ran for Congress.

Despite the political successes for gay causes, some people felt left behind.

Sylvia Rivera, the activist who cofounded STAR House, criticized gay-rights groups for ignoring the struggles of nonwhite gay and transgender people. Many of them ended up in jail, where they were beaten by guards and other inmates. Trans people were not even welcome in some gay bars.

At the 1973 Christopher Street Liberation Day rally, Sylvia told the crowd: "Your gay brothers and your gay sisters who are in jail . . . write me, every . . . week, and ask for your help. And you all don't do a . . . thing for them."

Harvey Milk (1930–1978)

One of the first openly gay politicians was a man named Harvey Milk. Born in a small New York town, Milk knew he was gay by high school. But he kept his personal life private until much later.

Harvey moved to San Francisco in 1972 and opened a camera shop in the Castro neighborhood. He became involved in the gay community. He was known as the "Mayor of Castro Street." In 1977, he was elected to the San Francisco Board of Supervisors.

Tragically, on November 27, 1978, Harvey Milk was shot and killed by Dan White, a disturbed former coworker. White had assassinated George Moscone, the San Francisco mayor, just moments before. The murders were partly over a dispute about a gay-rights law, which White opposed.

Before his death, Milk had spoken about the importance of coming out of the closet and living openly: "If a bullet should enter my brain," he said,

"let that bullet destroy every closet door."

Lesbian activists not only had to fight *homophobia*—the fear and hatred of gay people— they also had to fight for their rights as women. This was not an easy task.

The late 1960s and 1970s were an important time for women's rights. At the forefront was the National Organization for Women (NOW), cofounded by Betty Friedan. But Friedan worried that lesbians would hurt the women's rights cause. She made it clear that they were not welcome in her organization.

Betty Friedan in the 1970s

Queer people picket outside the White House on Armed Forces Day, 1965.

Mattachine Society "Sip-In" at the bar Julius', 1966

Police officers push back the crowd during the Stonewall uprising, June 1969.

A hand-painted message from the Mattachine Society pleading for order after the Stonewall uprising

Young people celebrate outside the boarded-up Stonewall Inn.

Damaged items inside the Stonewall Inn after riots

People hold signs during the first Stonewall anniversary march, New York, 1970.

A large crowd honors the anniversary of the Stonewall riots, 1971.

Fourth annual Gay Pride Day March, 1973

American gay rights activist Craig Rodwell

Politician Harvey Milk (left) and San Francisco mayor George Moscone

Members of PFLAG (Parents and Friends of Lesbians and Gays)
march in the New York Pride Parade, 1983.

Larry Kramer, founder of ACT UP, 1989

A mile-long rainbow flag was made in 1994 to commemorate
the twenty-fifth anniversary of the Stonewall uprising.

The National AIDS Memorial Quilt on display in Washington, DC, 1996

Del Martin (left) and Phyllis Lyon, cofounders of
the Daughters of Bilitis, are the first same-sex couple
to be married in San Francisco, 2008.

The Stonewall Inn is dedicated as a national monument, June 2016.

Newlyweds stand outside the Stonewall Inn, June 2016.

A large vigil held outside the Stonewall Inn for
Pulse nightclub shooting victims, 2016

President Barack Obama presents Ellen DeGeneres with
the Presidential Medal of Freedom, 2016.

RuPaul strikes a pose after being honored with a star on
the Hollywood Walk of Fame, 2018.

Danica Roem (center), the first openly transgender person elected to
statewide office, prepares to deliver her victory speech in Virginia, 2018.

Still, in 1973, gay-rights activists celebrated a major victory when the American Psychiatric Association finally declared that homosexuality was *not* a mental illness. (This would not be the case for transgender individuals until 2012.)

It was official: Gay people were *not* sick.

But tragically, in the 1980s, a real illness—a terrible one—began to kill many gay people: AIDS.

Psychiatrists, in a Shift, Declare Homosexuality No Mental Illness

CHAPTER 7
Crisis

HIV is a virus that attacks the immune system. The immune system is the body's natural defense against illness. If untreated, HIV can turn into AIDS. AIDS makes a person's body so weak, it can no longer fight off infections.

HIV/AIDS is a sexually transmitted disease. It can also be spread by using unclean hypodermic needles, so drug users are at risk. AIDS can affect anyone, not just LGBTQ+ people. But at first, it was almost only gay men who were dying from the disease.

People know a lot about AIDS today, including how to prevent one person from passing it to another. And those living with AIDS can manage their symptoms with medications. But in 1981, no one knew AIDS existed.

That spring, seemingly healthy gay men around the country began to fall ill. Purple spots appeared on their bodies. They experienced horrible night sweats. They lost a lot of weight. Common colds developed into serious cases of pneumonia. And no one was getting better.

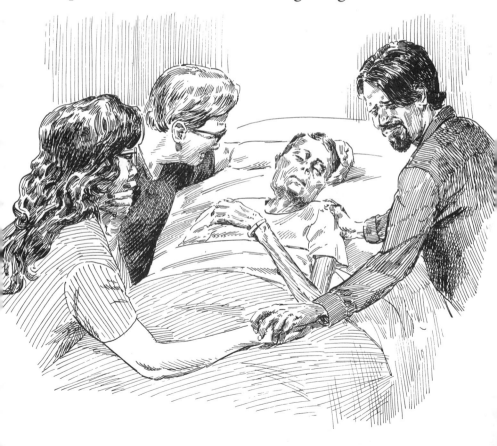

In response to this disaster, the Gay Men's Health Crisis (GMHC) was founded in New York in 1982. GMHC volunteers provided care for people living with AIDS. It soon grew to become the nation's largest gay organization.

"You Are Not Alone," poster from the GMHC

GMHC published newsletters and sent them to doctors and hospitals across the country, and worked to educate the queer community about the disease. In 1986, the GMHC held its first annual AIDS Walk, raising more than $700,000 for HIV/AIDS research. Thirty years and thirty walks later, $150 million had been raised.

More than fifty thousand Americans had AIDS by the end of 1987. Only two thousand had survived. By 1992, more than a quarter million Americans had AIDS. The annual Pride March began to feel more like a funeral procession for all these lost friends.

The AIDS Memorial Quilt

In June 1987, San Francisco activist Cleve Jones joined with others to create the NAMES Project Foundation. They began sewing squares to make a quilt honoring friends who had died from AIDS. Soon, people around the country started sending their own squares and panels.

By October, the quilt was publicly displayed on the National Mall in Washington, DC. With nearly two thousand pieces, it was bigger than a football field. More panels were added the following year. As the quilt toured the country, it raised money to help those living with AIDS.

The quilt now features nearly fifty thousand panels and weighs more than fifty tons!

Not until 1987, after so many had died of the disease, did President Ronald Reagan mention AIDS in public. During his presidency, funding for scientists trying to find a cure for the disease was cut. President George H. W. Bush continued these policies.

It was time, once again, for the LGBTQ+ community to ACT UP. The AIDS Coalition to Unleash Power (known as ACT UP) formed in 1987. The group included queer men, their straight allies, and many lesbians.

ACT UP put pressure on the government, the medical community, and drug companies to find a cure. Activists spilled the ashes of friends who had died from AIDS onto the lawn at the White House. "History will recall," they chanted, "Reagan and Bush did nothing at all!"

In 1992, Bill Clinton was elected president. "We're all part of the same community," Clinton said. "We'd better start behaving as if we are." The government now provided hundreds of millions of dollars for AIDS research. Three years later, new drugs kept the disease from getting worse. The number of deaths began to decline.

Today, there are medications that can all but prevent one person from giving HIV to another person.

Bill Clinton

Other medications help people living with HIV to lead a normal life. Unlike in the 1980s, HIV/AIDS is no longer a death sentence.

Still, every year, more than thirty thousand new cases of HIV occur in the United States—and thousands die of AIDS-related illnesses. Poorer communities are hit the hardest.

In 2016, an estimated 36.7 million people were living with HIV/AIDS around the world. More than 60 percent lived in sub-Saharan Africa. Some countries are working hard to cut the rate of infection, but others are not. Overall, year by year, new cases of HIV have slowed down. Still, it is an ongoing battle that everyone, especially world leaders, must take seriously.

Silence = Death

ACT UP's motto was "Silence = Death." It appeared under a pink triangle symbol. During the Holocaust in World War II, Nazi Germany arrested one hundred thousand people for the "crime" of bring gay. Fifteen thousand were sent to concentration camps. To identify them as gay people, they were made to wear pink triangles on their camp uniform. As many as 60 percent of these prisoners died.

CHAPTER 8
Out and Proud

Throughout the 1990s and into the twenty-first century, LGBTQ+ people have continued fighting for their rights. During this time, they began winning something more personal than political: people's hearts and minds.

Harvey Milk had spoken passionately about the importance of coming out. And in the years following Stonewall, and Milk's death, many LGBTQ+ people did just that. Then in 1988, October 11 was designated National Coming Out Day. For many more people now, a queer person was no longer someone

The logo by Keith Haring designed for National Coming Out Day

to fear or hate. Queer people were your relatives, friends, and coworkers. Yes, some families continued to reject queer family members. However, more and more were accepting: Here was the same sister, son, grandchild they had always loved. Nothing had changed except the knowledge that their relative was queer.

LGBTQ+ people in the public eye began coming out, too.

Ellen DeGeneres is an out lesbian who now hosts a beloved daily talk show watched by millions. Ellen came out in 1997 on the cover of *TIME* magazine alongside the headline: "Yep, I'm gay." At the time, she starred in her own TV sitcom. Two weeks later, Ellen's character on the show came out. Forty-four million tuned in.

Will & Grace was a TV comedy that aired

Main cast of the show *Will & Grace*

from 1998 to 2006. (It returned in 2017.) The show starred two openly gay men in its cast of characters. It was a top-rated sitcom for years.

In 1993, an openly gay drag queen named RuPaul took the world by storm with the dance hit "Supermodel (You Better Work)." Three years later, Ru hosted a talk show on VH1 that ran for one  hundred episodes. He has hosted *RuPaul's Drag Race*, a popular reality-TV competition for drag queens, since 2009.

The American public's views on LGBTQ+ people have changed a great deal. In 1996, the year before Ellen came out, just 27 percent of Americans supported same-sex marriage. By 2017, that number had grown to 64 percent.

Vice President Joe Biden made headlines in 2012 by supporting same-sex marriage. "I think *Will & Grace* probably did more to educate the American public than almost anything anybody's ever done so far," he said. "People fear that which is different. Now they're beginning to understand."

As many as three million children in the United States are being raised by LGBTQ+ parents. While they may still face discrimination and bullying, acceptance of these families has also risen over time. And in 2016, a Supreme Court ruling legalized adoption by same-sex parents nationwide.

That same year, President Barack Obama spoke about the changing times when he presented Ellen DeGeneres with the Presidential Medal of Freedom. "It's easy to forget now, when we've come so far . . . just how much courage was required for Ellen to come out on the most public of stages almost twenty years ago."

Ellen DeGeneres receiving the Presidential Medal of Freedom

Adam Rippon

The world has indeed come a long way. From pro sports stars like Olympic figure skater Adam Rippon and basketball player Jason Collins, to our elected leaders, queer people are more out and proud than ever before. Annise Parker was Houston, Texas's first openly lesbian mayor for six years. Kate Brown of Oregon was the nation's first openly bisexual governor. In 2017, Virginia's Danica Roem became the first openly transgender person elected to state government. And in 2018, voters in Colorado elected Jared Polis, the nation's first openly gay governor.

Danica Roem

The Rainbow Flag

Perhaps the most recognizable symbol of the LGBTQ+ community is the rainbow flag, also known as the Pride flag. Each color symbolizes something: red for life, orange for healing, yellow for sunlight, green for nature, blue for peace, and purple for spirit. The flag was designed in 1978 by Gilbert Baker, a friend of Harvey Milk's. In 1994, Baker organized the creation of a mile-long rainbow flag—the largest in the world—to commemorate the twenty-fifth anniversary of Stonewall.

CHAPTER 9
The Struggle Continues

After the Supreme Court legalized same-sex marriage in 2015, some officials in the South refused to give marriage licenses to same-sex couples. Kim Davis, a county clerk in Kentucky, said she was acting "under God's authority." She was eventually jailed for five days.

Kim Davis

Some states have passed laws allowing businesses to refuse services to LGBTQ+ people if doing so goes against the owner's religious beliefs. These anti-LGBTQ+ laws will be challenged in the courts, just as they have been since the 1960s.

Many LGBTQ+ children still experience rejection at home, at school, and at their places of worship. Some are kicked out by their families. Others run away. About 40 percent of homeless youth are LGBTQ+, a very high proportion. LGBTQ+ kids are also five times more likely to attempt suicide than their straight peers.

The LGBTQ+ community also continues to face terrible violence.

One night in 2016, a gunman opened fire at Pulse, an Orlando, Florida, nightclub. Pulse was popular with LGBTQ+ Latin people and their friends. Like the Stonewall Inn, Pulse was a very special place for the local queer community. It was supposed to be a safe space to gather and have fun. Forty-nine people were killed that night.

In 2017, twenty-nine transgender people—most of them nonwhite women—were murdered nationwide, the most ever recorded at the time. In 2017, there were fifty-two hate-based homicides, the deadliest year for LGBTQ+ people on record.

Memorial outside of Pulse nightclub, Orlando, Florida

Matthew Shepard (1976–1998)

On October 7, 1998, Matthew Shepard, a twenty-one-year-old college student, met two guys at a gay bar in Laramie, Wyoming. The men offered Matthew a ride home.

Instead, they drove him to a field, where they beat and robbed him, tied him to a fence, and left him to die. Matthew was found unconscious the next day; he died on October 12.

In 2009, the Hate Crimes Prevention Act was signed into law. A *hate crime* is a crime committed against someone because of their sexual identity, race, or religion. The new law made hate crimes against LGBTQ+ people a federal crime.

Despite the dangers and challenges, the world has changed for the better since Stonewall. Many organizations have formed to help LGBTQ+ youth. Support groups have built shelters, given out scholarships, and started clubs in schools. The message of these programs is clear: You are not alone, and you are worthy of love and respect.

The Trevor Project launched in 1998. It featured the first nationwide suicide prevention hotline for LGBTQ+ youth.

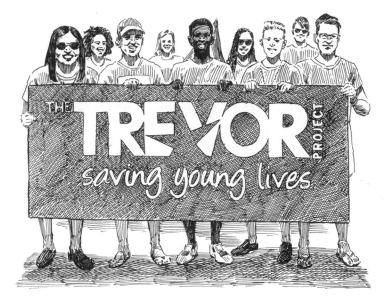

In 2010, gay writer-activist Dan Savage cofounded It Gets Better. Its mission was to save lives by preventing suicides among young people. LGBTQ+ adults, many of them famous, shared their childhood stories online. They promised viewers that while life as an LGBTQ+ kid can be really hard, it really does get better. The videos on the It Gets Better website have been viewed more than fifty million times.

Dan Savage

Born This Way

Many other celebrities have expressed their love and support for the LGBTQ+ community. Pop superstar Lady Gaga's song "Born This Way" assures listeners that they were born beautiful and special—and just who they were meant to be. "Just love yourself and you're set," she sings. You were "born to be brave." While medical professionals today say that many things determine whether someone will be queer, scientific studies of gay men's DNA appear to support the idea that queer people are likely born that way.

On June 24, 2016, President Barack Obama made history by dedicating the Stonewall Inn, Christopher Park, and the surrounding streets and sidewalks as the Stonewall National Monument. It was the first time a national landmark to honor LGBTQ+ history had been established.

"I believe our national parks should reflect the full story of our country," he said. "That we are stronger together. That out of many, we are one."

Timeline of Stonewall and the LGBTQ+ Rights Movement

1934 — Stonewall Inn Restaurant opens on Christopher Street

1950 — Harry Hay founds the Mattachine Society

1955 — Lesbian society Daughters of Bilitis founded

1965 — First "Annual Reminder" protest in Philadelphia

1966 — "Sip-In" held at Julius' and three other New York City bars

1967 — Gay people permitted by law to be served at bars

— Stonewall Inn opens as a gay bar on March 18

1968 — New York law banning same-sex dancing overturned

1969 — Police raid the Stonewall Inn the morning of June 28; clashes with protesters rock the neighborhood for days

— Stonewall closes in October

1970 — First annual Christopher Street Liberation Day march

1973 — American Psychiatric Association declares homosexuality is not a mental illness

1978 — Rainbow flag created by San Francisco artist Gilbert Baker

1981 — People (mostly gay men, at first) begin to die from AIDS

1987 — AIDS Quilt displayed on the National Mall

1993 — Stonewall Inn reopens as a gay bar and remains open to this day

1997 — TV star and comedian Ellen DeGeneres comes out

2004 — Massachusetts becomes first state to allow same-sex marriage

2015 — Same-sex marriage legalized nationwide in the USA

2016 — Stonewall National Monument is dedicated

Timeline of the World

1933 — Prohibition ends in the United States

1935 — In Nazi Germany, law is changed to make it easier to arrest queer people

1951 — Sally Ride, first American woman to go to space, is born

1954 — US Supreme Court declares segregation in public schools unconstitutional

1962 — Andy Warhol exhibits iconic *Campbell's Soup Cans* painting

1966 — National Organization for Women (NOW) is founded

1967 — Aretha Franklin's song "Respect" tops the charts

1968 — *Star Trek* airs American TV's first interracial kiss

1969 — Neil Armstrong becomes first person to walk on the moon

— Woodstock music festival held in Bethel, New York

1970 — At Kent State University in Ohio, four students are killed while protesting the Vietnam War

1973 — World Trade Center towers open in New York City

1981 — Lady Diana Spencer marries Charles, Prince of Wales

1982 — San Francisco Dodgers outfielder Glenn Burke is first pro baseball player to publicly come out of the closet

1986 — Lady Gaga is born in New York City

1991 — World Wide Web opens to the public

2003 — US troops and allies invade Iraq

2017 — Danica Roem becomes first openly transgender American elected to statewide political office

Bibliography

*Books for young readers

*Alsenas, Linas. *Gay America: Struggle for Equality.* New York: Amulet Books, 2008.

*Bausum, Ann. *Stonewall: Breaking Out in the Fight for Gay Rights.* New York: Viking, 2015.

"Harvey Milk," July 29, 2016, https://www.biography.com/people/harvey-milk-9408170.

Davis, Kate, and David Heilbroner, directors. *American Experience: Stonewall Uprising.* Boston: WGBH Educational Foundation, 2011.

Eaklor, Vicki L. *Queer America: A People's GLBT History of the United States.* New York: The New Press, 2011.

Resources

GLAAD

www.glaad.org: Gay and Lesbian Alliance Against Defamation.

GLSEN

www.glsen.org: Formerly known as the Gay, Lesbian, & Straight
    Education Network, GLSEN champions LGBT issues in K–12
    education.

GSA Network

www.gsanetwork.org: Helps LGBTQ+ students and straight allies
    organize GSA (gay-straight alliance) clubs to create safer schools.

It Gets Better Project

www.itgetsbetter.org

PFLAG

www.pflag.org: Parents, Families and Friends of Lesbians and Gays.

The Trevor Project

www.thetrevorproject.org: Provides information to LGBTQ+ youth
    through the Trevor Support Center and TrevorChat features,
    as well as a suicide prevention hotline.